Kids' Guide to Government

National
Government

REVISED EDITION

capstone

©2000, 2010, 2016 Heinemann Library
an imprint of Capstone Global Library, LLC
Chicago, Illinois

To contact Capstone Global Library, please
call 800-747-4992, or visit our website
www.mycapstone.com

Edited by Megan Cotugno
Designed by Ryan Frieson and Tony Miracle
Maps by Mapping Specialists
Picture research by Tracy Cummins and Heather Mauldin
Originated by Dot Gradations

**Library of Congress Cataloging-in-Publication Data is
available on the Library of Congress website.**
ISBN: 978-1-4846-3812-5 (paperback)

Acknowledgments
The author and publishers are grateful to the following
for permission to reproduce copyright material:
p. 5 Shutterstock/©Arvind Balaraman; p. 6 Jupiter
Images/©Royalty Free; p. 7 Getty Images/©Hulton
Archive; p. 10 Getty Images/©Alex Wong; p. 11 Associated
Press/©Kevork Djansezian; p. 13 Associated Press/©Doug
Mills; p. 14 Library of Congress, Prints & Photographs
Division/©National Child Labor Committee Collection; p.
15 Shutterstock/©Kent Weakley; p. 17 Newscom/©ZUMA
Press/The Washington Times; p. 18 Associated Press/©Susan
Walsh; p. 19 United States Senate; p. 20 Getty Images/ ©Mark
Wilson; p. 21 Collection of the U.S. House of Representatives;
p. 22 Associated Press/©Jose Luis Magana; p. 23 Associated
Press/©Dennis Cook; p. 24 Newscom/©Everett Collection;
p. 26 Getty Images/©AFP/Tim Sloan; p. 27 Associated
Press/©Matt York; p. 28 Newscom/©ZUMA Press/James
Berglie; p. 29 Newscom/©Reuters/Jim Young

Cover photograph reproduced with permission of Associated
Press/©J. Scott Applewhite.

We would like to thank Dr. John Allen Williams for his
invaluable help in the preparation of this book.

Printed and bound in the United States of America.
082018   000875

Contents

Some words are shown in bold, **like this**. You can find out
what they mean by looking in the glossary.

What Is Government?

A government is an organization of people that directs the actions of a nation, state, or community. A government has the **authority** and power to make, carry out, and **enforce** laws. It can also settle disagreements about those laws.

An important purpose of the United States government is to protect individual rights. In the United States, each person can believe what he or she wishes. People have the right to hold meetings and express opinions—even if these opinions disagree with actions of the government. People can choose their friends and the organizations they belong to.

The capital of the United States of America is Washington, D.C. Most government activities take place there.

The Capitol building, where Congress meets, is located in Washington, D.C.

The people who make up the national government of the United States of America work primarily in the nation's capital, the District of Columbia, also known as Washington, D.C.

The United States government has a responsibility to make sure that people are allowed to vote and to ask the government to change any laws they think are unfair.

In the United States, the national government's power comes from the U.S. Constitution. The Constitution is a document that describes—and places limits on—the powers of the national government. The Constitution gives the national government the power to raise a military force for defense, to collect **taxes**, and to make **economic** rules.

The United States government must make sure people can choose the kind of work they want to do and can own property.

The Constitution

The Constitution states that the United States government was formed by the people, and that its power comes from the people. This type of government is called a democracy. In a democracy, people elect, or choose, their leaders. In the United States, citizens choose who will be our national president and vice president. They also choose who will represent them in Washington, D.C. Perhaps more importantly, citizens can remove from office a person in government who is not meeting his or her responsibilities.

The people who wrote the U.S. Constitution wanted to make sure that the national government did not have too much power. The U.S. Constitution gives some powers to the national government and other powers to state governments. Some powers, such as the power to tax, are shared by both state and national governments. This is called a **federal** system of government.

Ancient Greeks and Romans each established a form of democracy for their governments. In ancient Rome, the Roman Senate exercised power by advising the government's leaders.

The U.S. Constitution is the world's oldest written constitution in use today.

The first Roman Senate house, or *curia*, was built in 670 BCE.
Above, a group of Romans **debate** during an **election** in 50 BCE.

Federal Powers	State Powers
make **treaties** with other nations	vote on constitutional amendments
provide for national defense	decide on voting requirements
collect taxes on goods from other countries	hold elections
print **currency**, **mint** coins	keep powers not given to the national government

The U.S. Constitution can be changed, or amended. An **amendment** must be ratified—agreed to—by two-thirds of the states. In more than 200 years, the Constitution has been amended 27 times.

Separation of Powers

The people who wrote the U.S. Constitution wanted to make sure that the leaders of the government did not have too much power. The writers spread the power among three separate branches of government that work together to govern the country. This is called **separation of powers**.

The executive branch is led by the president of the United States. This part of the government is responsible for making sure the laws are carried out, or executed.

The legislative branch is made up of the people in the Senate and the House of Representatives. Together, the Senate and the House of Representatives are called the United States Congress. The legislative branch makes the laws.

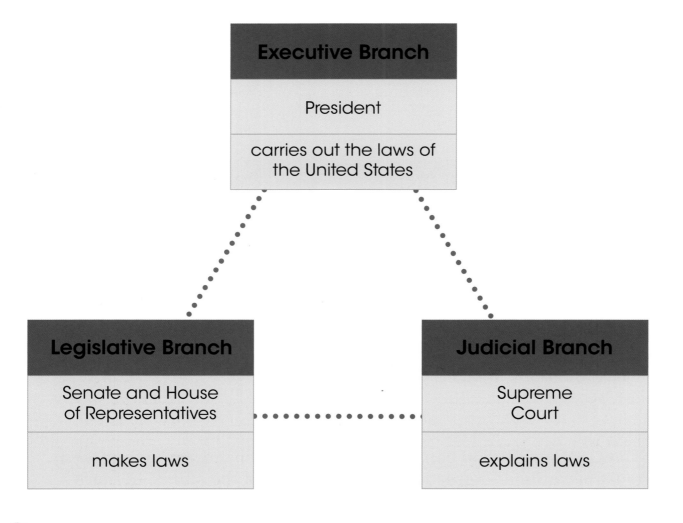

Executive Branch

President

carries out the laws of the United States

Legislative Branch

Senate and House of Representatives

makes laws

Judicial Branch

Supreme Court

explains laws

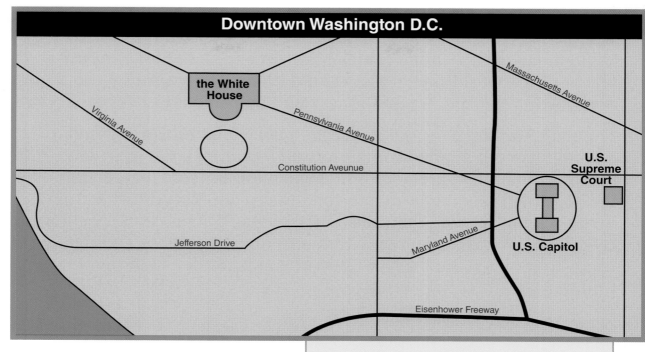

Downtown Washington D.C.

the White House

Virginia Avenue

Pennsylvania Avenue

Massachusetts Avenue

Constitution Aveunue

U.S. Supreme Court

Jefferson Drive

Maryland Avenue

U.S. Capitol

Eisenhower Freeway

The Capitol, the Supreme Court, and the White House are near each other in Washington, D.C.

The third branch is the judicial branch, which is led by the Supreme Court. The judges—called justices—of the Supreme Court explain the laws and decide if any laws go against the Constitution.

Each branch of the government has its own job to do, but the three branches have to work together. The people who wrote the Constitution were very careful to make sure that each branch of the government could check up on the others. A system called **checks and balances** keeps different parts of the government from having too much power.

The president, for example, can veto, or reject, a law passed by Congress and force Congress to pass it again with a larger **majority**. The Supreme Court justices serve for life, but Congress makes the rules for the Supreme Court. Also, Congress can remove a justice from the Supreme Court, or even the president, if it decides he or she is not acting properly. On the other hand, the Supreme Court can stop a law passed by Congress if it decides that the law is against the Constitution.

The Executive Branch

The president of the United States is known around the world as the head of the United States government and **chief executive** of one of the world's most powerful nations. The president's actions are widely reported in newspapers and on radio and television.

The Constitution gives the president power and **authority** that no other person in government has. For example, the president is the commander-in-chief of the armed forces. This means that the president has the power to send the Army, Navy, Marines, or Air Force into battle. The president also has the power to negotiate **treaties** with other countries. Some treaties are about ending a war. Others may be about the sale of goods produced in the United States to other countries.

President Barack Obama addresses members of Congress in 2009.

The Constitution calls for the president to let Congress know how the nation is doing. Once a year, during the State of the Union address, the president talks about achievements the country has made or the problems it faces. The president also makes suggestions for solving problems and asks Congress to consider these solutions.

The president may create special agencies to do jobs that are for the common good. These are offices that provide special kinds of help. People working for the Food and Drug Administration (FDA), for example, make sure the food we eat is free from disease. They also investigate new medicines to make sure they really work against an illness and will not cause harm.

The president may turn some jobs over to the vice president. According to the Constitution, if the president dies, the vice president takes over the position.

To be President of the United States a person must have been born in the United States, have lived in the country for at least 14 years, and be at least 35 years old.

Below, FDA workers test foods that could be contaminated with **salmonella**. It is the FDA's job to ensure that food consumed by the public is safe.

The President's Cabinet

The executive branch of government includes 15 departments whose leaders advise the president. Together, these leaders are known as the president's Cabinet. The president has the power to choose a person to head a department. The choice must be approved by the Senate.

Even though the Cabinet is not mentioned in the Constitution, it plays an important part in the government. Each person in the Cabinet heads up a different department and has the title of secretary. For example, there is a secretary of the treasury, a secretary of the interior, and a secretary of agriculture. Only the Department of Justice (which includes the Federal Bureau of Investigation, or FBI) is headed by someone not called a secretary. He or she is called the attorney general.

The President's Cabinet	
Secretary of state	Secretary of housing and urban development
Secretary of the treasury	Secretary of transportation
Secretary of defense	Secretary of homeland security
Secretary of the interior	Secretary of education
Secretary of agriculture	Secretary of energy
Secretary of commerce	Secretary of veterans' affairs
Secretary of labor	Attorney general
Secretary of health and human services	

Former President George W. Bush is shown meeting with his Cabinet in the Cabinet Room of the White House in 2002.

The responsibilities of the Cabinet are varied. For example, the Department of State works mostly with other nations to make sure that the **political** and **economic** interests of the United States are protected. The Department of Commerce works to keep the business interests of the nation healthy and strong. The Department of the Interior is responsible for how lands belonging to the **federal** government are used, protected, and maintained. It also oversees matters having to do with Native Americans.

In addition to printing **currency** and making coins, the Treasury Department is responsible for investigating **smuggling** and the printing of **counterfeit** money. The U.S. Secret Service, which protects the president and vice president and their families, is also a part of the Treasury Department.

The Legislative Branch

In the United States, men and women are elected to Congress to represent the people. These men and women form the legislative branch of our government. They are responsible for passing laws that make the nation run smoothly and fairly.

Some laws passed by Congress protect the rights of individuals. Others are for the common good. For example, they set aside land for national parks and make sure we have clean air and water. They send help to areas that have been flooded or damaged by storms.

> The United States Congress met for the first time on March 4, 1789.

Before Congress passed laws against child labor in the 1930s and 1940s, children as young as six worked from dawn to dusk, six days a week, in dangerous and dirty conditions.

The Capitol building in Washington, D.C., was completed in 1829. This view shows the inside of the building's domed ceiling.

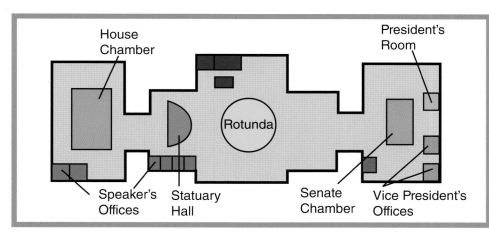

This map shows the layout of the Capitol building.

The Constitution gives Congress power and **authority** that no other branch of government has. For example, only Congress can declare war, borrow money, print currency, and establish taxes that working adults in the nation must pay.

There are more than 500 members of Congress. They spend a lot of time talking and trading ideas with one another. Each person tries to do the best for the people in his or her home area as well as for all the people in the country. People in Congress also try to do what their **political party** wants. Because Congress spends so much time **deliberating** over the many items brought before it, things may seem to work very slowly.

Congress

The U.S. Congress consists of two bodies, or groups, of people—the Senate and the House of Representatives. Both bodies meet in the United States Capitol in Washington, D.C.

The Senate is made up of 100 senators—two from each of the 50 states. Each senator represents his or her entire state. The people in each state elect their senators, who serve for **terms** of six years.

To be a senator, a person must be at least 30 years old and have been a U.S. citizen for at least nine years. Representatives must be at least 25 years old and have been a U.S. citizen for seven years. The senator or representative must live in the state that elects him or her.

The House of Representatives is made up of 435 voting members elected for a term of two years from **congressional districts** in each state. The number of districts a state has depends on the **population** of the state, which is measured every ten years in a **census**. For example, people in Kansas elect four representatives to serve in the House, while the people in California elect 53 representatives.

Every 10 years, the U.S. Census Bureau counts the total U.S. population and makes adjustments to the number of representatives each state has. Some states may gain representatives, while other states may lose some. However, the total number of representatives in the House remains 435.

California: 53 representatives

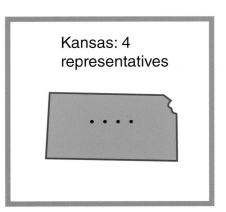

Kansas: 4 representatives

Senators and representatives can be elected for many terms. Some states tried to pass laws that limited the number of years a person may serve, but in 1995, the Supreme Court ruled that states cannot set term limits for Congress members.

Congress meets throughout most of the year, from early January to late fall (early fall in election years). While Congress is in session, members live in Washington, D.C., but return to their states or districts as much as possible. When Congress closes, senators and representatives usually return home.

Senator Strom Thurmond (1902–2003) of South Carolina was 100 years old in 2002 and had served in Congress for 47 years and 5 months, breaking all records for service.

During their **campaigns**, people who want to serve in Congress try to meet as many voters as possible.

The Senate

The Constitution gives the Senate important power and authority. In the system of checks and balances, the Senate must approve any treaties the president makes with other countries and do so with a two-thirds majority. It also has the power to approve the president's choices for Cabinet members, Supreme Court justices, and **ambassadors** to other countries.

The vice president of the United States acts as the president of the Senate. However, the vice president rarely presides over the discussion or **debate** in Senate. If there is a tie when the senators vote on an issue, the vice president can vote and break the tie.

The Senate can appoint one of its members to be president *pro tempore* (president for a time). This person presides over the Senate when the vice president is away. They are also third in line for the presidency.

West Virginia's Senator Robert Byrd took over as president *pro tempore* during a 2008 session of the Senate.

Above the chamber is a balcony, called a gallery. Here, visitors who come to visit the Capitol can watch the Senate at work.

The place where the Senate meets is called the Senate chamber. It has 100 desks that face the front of the room. Senators of the same political party sit on the same side of the room.

The vice president sits at the front and center, facing the senators. Secretaries and recorders sit below him. They keep a record of what happens in the Senate. In addition, there are clerks and aides who help the senators keep track of the business of the day.

The Senate chooses someone to be their U.S. Senate sergeant-at-arms. This person helps protect Congress members. The sergeant-at-arms also plans special ceremonies and **escorts** the president and visiting heads of state when they come to speak to Congress.

The House of Representatives

The House of Representatives is sometimes just called the House. This branch has power and **authority** that no other part of government receives. Only the House can write laws that collect taxes. Also, if a high government official, such as a president or federal judge, does something that does not seem right, the House must decide whether to put that person on trial before the Senate.

The members of the House of Representatives choose one member to be the Speaker of the House. He or she oversees any debate in the House. Because there are so many representatives, much of the work of the House goes on in committees.

The Speaker of the House administers the oath of office to House members.

The representatives, sometimes called congressmen and congresswomen, sit at desks in the large chamber. Desks and tables at the front are used by secretaries, recorders, clerks, aides, and an official called the **parliamentarian**. All these people keep track of what happens in the House.

The members of the House choose one person (not a member of the House) to be the sergeant-at-arms. He or she keeps order in the House during debate. The sergeant-at-arms is also in charge of the Mace, the symbol of power in the House of Representatives.

As in the Senate, a balcony surrounds most of the House chamber, from which visitors can watch the activity when Congress is in session.

While the House is in session, the Mace sits on a marble table, called a pedestal, to the right of the Speaker of the House. But when the House is in committee, the Mace is moved to a lower pedestal.

The Mace of the House is carried into the chamber each day by the House sergeant-at-arms.

Committees

There are many areas that need the attention of the legislators in Congress. In order to get all the work done, both the House and the Senate divide their work by forming small groups called committees. Each committee deals with just one part of Congress's job.

Both the Senate and the House have their own committees. There are a few committees in which senators and representatives work together. These are called joint committees. Many committees work on passing new laws. Some committees investigate events that interest the government. There are permanent, or standing, committees and committees formed for just a short time.

Standing committees in the Senate and the House include:
- Agriculture
- Appropriations
- Banking
- Foreign Relations
- Judiciary
- Small Business
- Veterans' Affairs

A senator speaks during a subcommittee on disaster relief.

Governors speak to a Senate Appropriations committee relating to hurricane relief for the Gulf Coast region devastated by Hurricane Katrina.

Each committee lets the public know what they are working on and what kinds of laws they are thinking of making. People who have an interest in what a committee is doing can ask to speak to the committee. Sometimes a committee invites people to speak to them in a session called a hearing.

People can meet with the committee on agriculture to ask for help for farmers. Other people might urge a committee to pass laws against owning guns. Committee members talk among themselves and **deliberate** about what was said at the hearings. Finally they reach a decision about whether or not Congress as a whole should pass or change a law.

One of the most important committees in both the House and the Senate is the Appropriations committee. This committee sets aside, or appropriates, money for projects approved by Congress or recommended by other committees.

The Judicial Branch

The judicial branch of government is made up of judges, or justices, who serve on the U.S. Supreme Court and the judges in other federal district courts. The president appoints, or chooses, judges to serve in these courts, but the Senate must approve each appointment.

The Constitution gives responsibilities to the judicial branch that the other branches do not have. It is the responsibility of the judicial branch to make decisions concerning whether laws that Congress has passed agree with the Constitution.

The nine justices of the Supreme Court sit at this raised table, called a bench.

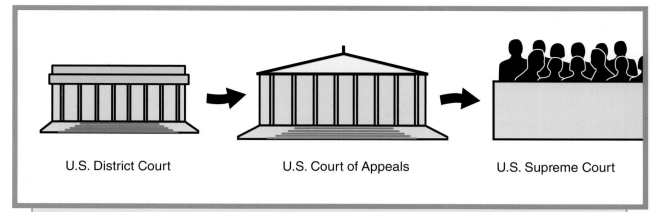

U.S. District Court   U.S. Court of Appeals   U.S. Supreme Court

A case in the federal court system starts out at a district court. Each state has at least one federal district court. One is also located in Washington, D.C.

The 12 regional courts of appeals are often referred to as circuit courts. Early in our nation's history, the judges of the courts of appeals visited each of the courts in a region in a certain order, or circuit, until they returned to where they had started. The judges, who traveled on horseback, were called circuit riders.

Laws passed by cities and states must not disagree with or contradict the laws set by the Constitution. The Supreme Court has the responsibility to determine whether or not a law is constitutional.

Federal courts may also hear cases in which the United States government or one of its officers is either **suing** someone or is being sued. The federal courts may also decide cases in which one or more states disagree with each other. For example, one state might sue a neighboring state, claiming that state is polluting the air. The federal courts may also hear cases in which an ordinary person brings a case against a state.

People who are unhappy with a decision made by a district court can ask one of the 12 courts of appeals to hear the case. If they are still unhappy with the decision, they can ask the U.S. Supreme Court to hear the case.

The Supreme Court

The Supreme Court of the United States is the nation's top court. Once a justice is appointed to the Supreme Court, he or she serves for life. However, a justice may resign if he or she is ill or wishes to retire.

The president chooses one Supreme Court justice to be the leader, or chief justice. The chief justice is in charge of how the Supreme Court is run. The other eight men and women are called associate justices.

> The Supreme Court meets from the first Monday of October through June.

The Supreme Court justices in 2005. Back row: Sonia Sotomayor, Stephen G. Breyer, Samuel Anthony Alito, Jr., and Elena Kagan. Front row: Clarence Thomas, Antonin Scalia, Chief Justice John G. Roberts, Jr., Anthony M. Kennedy, and Ruth Bader Ginsburg.

William O. Douglas served longer than any other Supreme Court justice. He served for 36 years, from 1939 until 1975.

In 1981 Sandra Day O'Connor was the first woman appointed to the Supreme Court. She retired in 2005.

During the year, the Supreme Court may be asked to listen more than 7,500 cases. Most of the time, the justices decide that a case is not important enough to take the time of the entire court.

However, the Supreme Court does listen to about 100 cases a year. All nine justices listen to each case brought to the Supreme Court while lawyers tell both sides of the issue. There are no witnesses and there is no **jury**. The justices deliberate with one another and reach what they think is the best decision by majority vote. Often the justices write out their opinions in important cases, so that people will understand their reasoning. All nine justices don't have to agree in order to reach a decision.

Paying for Government

It costs a lot of money to run the federal government. The Constitution says that only Congress has the power to raise money for the United States.

The salaries of the president, members of Congress, and the judges in the Supreme Court are paid by the government. Millions of workers in the different departments help the government run from one day to the next, and they all must be paid. People in the military must be paid. Every space shuttle, every meat inspection, every mile of federal highway must be paid for.

Each year, Congress and the president work together to make a **budget** for the government for the next year. Sometimes it takes a long time for them to reach agreement because they have very different ideas on the most important things to pay for.

President Barack Obama addresses the public with his team of economic advisors. The president and Congress must work hard to create a budget that benefits the U.S. public.

The government prints currency and places it in **circulation**. It collects money from different sources to pay its expenses.

No one, not even the president, can spend the country's money unless Congress first approves it.

Most of the money the government receives comes from taxes. In the United States, most tax is collected on what people earn for the work they do. This tax, called an income tax, is collected each year on April 15th. The federal government also collects taxes from businesses, but personal income tax brings in most of the government's money.

In some cases, the government places a tax on specific products. For example, there are federal taxes on gasoline. A few cents from each gallon of gas purchased goes to the federal government, and is used to build and maintain highways.

Sometimes the government spends more money on programs and improvements than it takes in. This difference leads to the **national debt**, which has been steadily rising over the years.

How Laws Are Made

The idea for a law can come from a citizen or group or from a person already in Congress. The idea must pass several tests before it can become a federal law.

1. A representative or a senator writes up the idea. At this point the idea is called a bill.

2. A bill written by a representative is presented to the House. A bill introduced by a senator is presented to the Senate.

3. A committee reads the bill and gathers information about how the bill might work as a law. The committee reports to the House (or Senate) on the details of the bill.

4. The House (or Senate) votes on the bill.

5. If the bill passes the vote, it is sent to the other part of Congress.

6. The Senate (or House) studies the bill and then takes a vote.

7. If the bill changes as it goes through the other part of Congress, a committee of representatives and senators work out the final wording of the bill.

8. The House and Senate vote on the final bill.

9. If the bill passes the vote, it is sent to the president to sign.

10. The president signs the bill and it becomes a law. The president can also veto the bill and send it back to Congress where it must be passed by a two-thirds vote in each house to become law.

Glossary

ambassador messenger or representative

amendment change to the Constitution, requiring two-thirds of the states to agree

authority the power to make people obey laws, to command obedience, or judge

budget plan describing the amount of money that will be spent and received during a given time

campaign organized effort to win election to public office

census count and gathering of information about a population; happens every ten years

checks and balances system that makes sure different parts of government cannot become stronger than other parts

chief executive top person in the executive branch

circulation in use

congressional districts areas of almost equal population that states are divided into for election purposes

counterfeit imitation that looks like the original

currency paper money and coins used in a country

debate to discuss arguments for and against something

deliberate to talk about in order to make a decision

economic having to do with money and resources

election process of making a choice by voting

enforce to make people obey

escort to go with or accompany

federal the central government of the United States. It also refers to a group of states that give up some power to a central government.

jury citizens who hear evidence in a lawsuit and reach a decision

majority the greater number or part; more than half the total

mint to manufacture coins

national debt money owed by the government

parliamentarian expert on the rules and conduct of a group of lawmakers

political having to do with government

political party group of people who have similar views about government

population total number of people living in a certain area

salmonella a type of bacteria that causes diarrhea; spread mostly by contaminated food

separation of powers system of government that distributes power among several branches and keeps each branch separate by making it illegal for officials in one branch to serve in another

smuggle to secretly bring into or take out of a country something that is illegal

sue to bring legal action against, to take to court

tax money required by the government for its support; may be based on property owned, money earned, or things bought

term length of time, set by law, served by an elected person

Find Out More

Reis, Ronald A. *The US Congress for Kids: A History of Lawmaking, Deal-Breaking, and Compromising, With 21 Activities.* Chicago: Chicago Review Press, 2014.

Krieg, Katherine. *Congress.* Vero Beach, Flo.: Rourke Educational Media, 2015.

Krull, Kathleen. *A Kids' Guide to America's Bill of Rights.* New York: Harper, an Imprint of HarperCollinsPublishers, 2015.

Turner, Juliette. *Our Constitution Rocks.* Grand Rapids, Mich.: Zondervan, 2012.

Index